HUMAN

Human:

Behind the Mask

CARLY REED

*A written memoir of spiritual growth
through recovery.*

Glory be to God.

CONTENTS

ꟼNTRODUCTION

You are stronger than you think.

Hi, my name is Carly Reed and I am taking off my mask in this poetry series in hopes to connect with and inspire you to fight the good fight and not give up. I almost did.

My hope is by sharing my struggle with addiction, body dysmorphia, and mental health, that someone will hear my story and decide to make a positive change, or at least consider the thought. That's one step in the right direction, and every step counts.

Don't be afraid to fail or take steps back. Life happens. The process of failing fosters humility, which is necessary for self-improvement; and failures can be a series of repeated attempts that eventually lead us to success. Finding the message within your mess can help you appreciate the experience instead of resenting it.

Living with no regrets is easier said than done. My only regret now is that I didn't ask for help sooner. I don't want my next regret to be not speaking up to help others.

I hope speaking out on my struggle with addiction can help others feel confident enough to embrace and love themselves, and realize we were all created uniquely by God with a purpose.

No matter what we may look like to the rest of the world, understanding and believing we are all His children and we are enough in His eyes, will hopefully prevent someone else from seeking comfort quietly and alone through substances like I did.

REMINDER

God gave you a purpose before anyone gave an opinion.

During recovery, and still to this day, every time I felt like I wanted to use, I write. For the first time in my life, I was evolving through self-discovery as I unpacked painful memories and fears — which I'd been masking with substances for years.

Written thoughts help me not run from my demons; instead I started facing them head-on, turning my experiences into words of thoughtful realizations. I found an outlet to connect with others by turning pain into a beautiful conceptualized format, poetry.

Each poetic concept was developed by spending time in my cravings and questioning why? Why do I want to use? Which substance do I want to use? What triggered this urge?

Questioning my urges, the why, helped me discover my 'how' — how to ride out the cravings and remain sober through writing.

Show Up & Tell

The opposite of addiction is connection

No longer living in substance-driven isolation

Words formatted from hurt
Pain can be purposeful if you let it

Grateful to God for guiding me

On this path, I'm forever learning

And the messages of lessons I speak through me

With hopes to inspire from vulnerability
and healing

Welcome to Carly's Sobriety Journey

Recover Out Loud

Forgiving ourselves can be harder
than forgiving someone else

Each day is a fresh start to become your best self

Empowerment to grow and improve

Recovering out loud, shared truth

Before it would burn, now it blooms

Happiness looks gorgeous on you

Words Have Power

Now I format my thoughts into words instead

Who knew pain could be so poetic

Handing you my heart from my chest

Taking off the bullet proof vest

Every challenge, victory, setback,
and step forward

Provides an opportunity of something
to be grateful for

God gives us gifts,

And His greatest one is Christ within

Words have power

They can shed or dim your light

I aim to radiate bright

"Do you have the gift of speaking? Then speak as though God Himself were speaking through you. Do you have the gift of helping others? Do it with all the strength and energy that God supplies. Then everything you do will bring glory to God through Jesus Christ. All glory and power to Him forever and ever! Amen."

1 PETER 4:11

Masked Series Intro

This series was written in October around Hallow-een to express the inner struggle with our demons and lies occurring behind our masks.

I was diagnosed with Borderline Personality Disorder, which can feel like Halloween daily — it's a consistent battle within and the masks being worn feel out of your control.

This series of poems shows a progression from hiding myself due to shame and stigmas around mental health and addiction (mask on), to embracing my uniqueness and stepping into my true identity, covered by God (mask off).

"So all of us who have had the veil removed can see and reflect the glory of the Lord. And the Lord — who is the Spirit — makes us more and more like Him as we are changed into His glorious image."

2 CORINTHIANS 3:18

Behind the Scenes

Of every mask there is a face
Of every face there is a story

Unintentionally playing a game
Strongholds taking center stage

Welcome to my masquerade
Emotional Russian roulette

Which one will I wear today?
I lost myself, who am I?

Spent so long in disguise
I lost myself, who am I?

Look alive on the outside
Underneath, emptiness inside
Obstruct your view, and mine
Barricades my face can hide behind
But not my eyes, they don't lie

Pull the curtains, exit stage

Intermission, costume change

Remove my masks for the world to see

A sensitive human being

Wearing my heart on my sleeve

Grateful for His love, grace and mercy

No longer masked, God covers me

His word releases me from
the sense of inadequacy

As I step in to my true identity

Lights on

Audience of one

GOODBYE

I'll smile and grin

It's to keep you out rather than let you in

Cover my sensitivity, keep it hidden

Beneath me — the feeling of crippling emotion

While showing the portrayal of perfection

Drawing an ever moving finish line of expectation

Masks are worn as a form of protection

They helped me manage,
and became my companions

But only I could feel their battle within me

And sometimes friends become enemies

Invisibly turning on me, internally

Rumination is always personal, pervasive

Focused on my shortcomings, purely negative

Relapsing repeatedly in my own head

Using masks as shields built walls
around my heart

They tumble down as I fall apart

Some things feel safe but keep you blind

It's myself I eventually didn't recognize

Time to say goodbye

Melt

Buried beneath shame and guilt,

Hiding my true self

These masks became glued to my face

Bound by ropes and chains

I pray they eventually melt away

Carefully listen to what I really have to say

Tongue and cheek,

Smoke and mirror speech

Do my words cut too deep?

Send a shiver down your spine

As you Reed between the lines

Some of my confessions, cringe-worthy

But self-expression is so liberating

Wonder if I'll ever truly be happy

For now, at least I feel free

Masks are a trap, for you and me

LABEL ME

A label that reads "don't help me"

Difficult to process emotion normally

Dysregulated internally

Triggers occur without warning

Brain firing consistent and rapidly

The worst of the past mentally reinforcing

Flashbacks repeatedly playing

Spiraling, splitting, it's happening

It feels like a horror movie

Living a nightmare inside

Lash out, Jekyll & Hyde

Distressful thoughts

It's not your fault

Dramatic reactions

Destructive patterns

Blank stare consumes my face

Distance and disassociate

Existing elsewhere in my mind that feels safe

Between reality and the void,
anywhere but this place

But it's myself I can't escape

Overcome by emptiness within

That's behind every sin

Label me HUMAN

Trade in my masks for His perspective

As I wear His affirmation and acceptance

Label me HUMAN.

At Rest Series Intro

This three-part series (chained, cleansed, at rest) was written to express the shift in recovery.

From being bound by substances (chained), to surrendering to sobriety (cleansed), and forgiving the past (rest).

"And because you belong to Him, the power of the life-giving Spirit has freed you from the power of sin that leads to death."

ROMANS 8:2

CHAINS

Undeniably bound by substances

The chains gripped me tight with sin

Perfect armor for protection

Never wanting to break them,

I liked living that way; no desire to change

Those chains numbed pain

Until one day, a hurricane

It felt like everything was crushed
& stripped away

First my house, no longer a home

Then my heart, left alone

How do I explain what it's like,

To want a temporary feeling more
than your own life?

To need that sensation to feel alive —

To not care if it were to all be over —

To forget what it's like to function sober —

To not recognize your own face in the mirror

Took a hard fall into habits I never thought

How am I not strong enough, to take a day off?

And resist the temptation —

This is no longer for recreation

Altered state of mind lifestyle

Last weapon in my arsenal:

Pray

As I begged to not continue to fall

I remember what it felt like when we really met,

He came to me right where I was at

He reminded me I'm never alone

He reminded me I am home

Right where I belong —

No longer wrapped in chains, just His arms

He told me, 'I love you as you are'

He helped me look up from the mess I was in

I took His hand, and slowly my recovery began

The chain links began to gently

Break off and fall away

My spirit strengthened

to resist my bodily weakness

of consistent cravings

Step work peels back the painful layers

I've been hiding behind

Unveiling the truth hurts every time

To the girl staring back at me in the mirror,
I apologize

Addiction is a disease — it's cunning & baffling

And every day is going to be a fight

For the rest of this life

Sacrifice

I surrender to my bondage breaker

Giving every temptation to Him in daily prayer

A communication that has been key

To honoring the greatest gift I've ever been given:

Sobriety

Living in freedom of His grace,

God works in mysterious ways

The Perfect Storm

Every grain of sand clinging to my skin

Represents some form of sin

Wearing my recognized rebellion

The sand feels like dirt as it sticks

And each bit depicts

Every pill swallowed, substance abused,
person used

I was hurting too

Take me off this course

Set to crash and burn

As I walk into the water

It rains down and I pray harder

Give me a spiritual shower

Wash me clean from my guilt and shame

As I make amends with my mistakes

Hands up to the sky

Tears fall from my eyes

I'm helpless against the tide
Every breaking wave that crashes
The ocean calms once it passes
Nature's amazingly adaptive

Like water changing form
Consider it a perfect storm
Thunder comes as it gets darker from above
When the light is lost, I too lose love

He reminds me the sun is in my heart
This is leading into a fresh start
To the old me, I send my distant regards

As I embrace the change
Wave after wave
It waters my faith

Gaining courage and patience, as I wait
To harvest this fruit

Slates don't get cleaned
Unless we wipe them new

SANDS OF TIME

Flip it again — another try;
Repeat of the same cycle,
it's like pressing rewind

Plot twist: a different script,
Changed the cast up a little bit
Few new characters came in
But we know how this will end
Adversities leading to self-destruction

Trapped inside an hourglass
Measuring repetitive moments as they pass

The sand piles, and sticks to me
Each grain, different feelings of a memory
The accumulation is getting heavy
As it clings to my mind and body

Stuck behind this clear barricade,
Repeating time in a cage

How to get out of my own way

Fracture the glass that's holding me back

Shattered fragments surround

Standing on messy and unfamiliar ground

How to manage without my old habits now

Grieving is dark and lonely,

Can't lift the heaviness of the remorse I carry

You found me where I hid,

In the midst of numbing with substances

Reaching out with a rescuing hand,

Together we wrote a new narrative

Getting sober is where it began

I respond in guilt and shame,

And you gently lifted the weight

As I am freed by Your grace

Led by spirit, guided by faith

To Your unconditional love, my heart awakes

In a new bed as I lay,

The sand grains of previous sin

Turn to flower petals from within

With a new perspective,

The past is no longer such a burden

It's quite beautiful from this angle

As I touch each petal,

They hold memories and lessons,
for which I am grateful

At peace with my past,

As I've learn to accept

My shortcomings and mistakes,

Laying in My Father's embrace

Surrounded by the beauty of my pain

Changed, restored, and safe

Reminding me as I'm finally at rest,

'I don't remember anything of your sin
once you repent'

Surrounded by the
beauty of my pain

TAILOR MADE SERIES INTRO

This three-part series is intended to express the struggle with body image and societal standards.

Becoming too focused on external appearance, looks, and status, can rot you on the inside.

My addiction amplified as I was chasing money and the 'American Dream' — I lost myself.

The message is, happiness isn't found through societal validation.

I was chasing external possessions and achievements to fill a void that only God can fill.

Only His presence can make us whole.

"Don't be concerned about the outward beauty of fancy hairstyles, expensive jewelry, or beautiful clothes. You should clothe yourselves instead with the beauty that comes from within, the unfading beauty of a gentle and quiet spirit, which is so precious to God."

1 PETER 3: 3-4

TAILOR MADE

Step onto the scale

You can't be serious

How'd I gain two pounds

over the weekend?

What's the cure for self hatred?

Learned the hard way, it wasn't substances

As an effort to heal and understand

Now I format my thoughts into words instead

Who knew pain could be so poetic

Every attempt to write this

Tears sit behind my eyelids

An apology to my body

With a bit of an explanation

Watching the most beautiful people
have children,

We were told we couldn't do that

So let's marry my career and collect possessions

Tangible objects, like kids, I'll even name them

Thought I had the perfect life plan

Combat feelings with substances and brands

Tainted by society standards

Sacrificing morals for appearance

No secret the world we live in

Places a heavy emphasis and attraction

On physical looks and status

Clutching my designer purse

Wrap the tape measure around my curves,

Do these numbers tell you my worth?

A reflection that's vacant in the mirror

With an empty stare, are you there?

Eyes glare, masking sadness

Body dysmorphia at it's finest

Hoping my body can forgive me

For filling it with toxins and verbal negativity

The names I called you, the self-harm endured

I didn't know how else to communicate my hurt

I've treated you like the enemy,

But we're supposed to be a team

I ask my body now if we can be friends

It said it's waited our whole life for this

Tells me it thinks I look perfect

Let's get comfortable in my own skin

Beauty isn't a size, what lies within?

Redirecting my focus on love and appreciation

Reminder that we're God's creation

He cares about our heart's condition

Each of us intricately made my Him,

With the purest of intention

To serve the Kingdom and live in good faith

Our jean size won't open Heaven's gates

SUPERFICIAL FEAST

Self-medicating, numbing to bury

Into the mental graveyard of real feelings

Emotions beneath the surface

Tombstones spell out reasons

Can I turn this burial ground into a garden?

Dig up the pain, prepare for healing

Sober entry into a brighter personal season

Got used to letting go like autumn, living recluse

Been mentally stuck in winter,
eager for spring to bloom

Frozen by hidden emotions, internally bruised

Cracked shell of a human, they resurface,
I can't move

Unknowingly planted new roots in open wounds

Overworked to afford solutions
for my inner issues

Substances and materialistic items
served as substitutes

Helped mask feelings and
avoid facing harsh truths

Least emotional risk, I did the math

Value things that can't hurt me, like people can

Seemed common sense,
love won't pay the mortgage

And there's zero calories in a Chanel bag

But that also means there's no sustenance

So much for the artificial bandages

Culture's standards are forever changing

And trends become outdated

Happiness isn't found through societal validation

Underneath the makeup and jewels,
Our body's use is to shelter our soul

Neglected to make the interior feel like home

Internal battles can't be won alone,
I found my solution that brought me back home

Only His presence makes me whole

Lost deeply in shallow thoughts

Naked vulnerability of a nocturnal heart

Witness how stars illuminate the dark

SPIRITUAL PRESCRIPTION

Vanity encompasses things we pursue that
won't last beyond this Earth

While we may admire one's physical aspects
or fancy assets, we may learn

Admirable body imagery in reverse,

How to illuminate from within

Scripture being the prescription

Taught me the truth about body image

Superficial feasting left my soul still hungry

Luke says, "You cannot serve God
and be enslaved to money"

Peter teaches against overemphasis
on outward appearance;
Beauty comes from within, it's a person's spirit

James reminds us physical looks eventually fade

Like a flower, ends up withering away

Matthew warns about storing valuables
here on Earth

Where moths eat, rusting and theft occurs

Romans tells us our body is a living sacrifice

And instructs us to be transformed by
a renewing of the mind

Instead of conforming to the world,
for it can blind

Human eyes

Impurities fill me inside

I'll work to improve but no longer do I deny

Perfectly imperfect, individual uniqueness

Starting with raw acceptance,

I am forever a work in progress

WEIGH IN

Tip the scale with my sin

The struggle lies within

Me versus myself, inner conflict

I'm shadowboxin'

I don't battle with anyone else

My fights are internal, amongst myself

Against the cravings of addiction

Against self-harm, negative body image

Against my personalities in competition

Trying to seek direction

We meet again, step in

Enter the ring wearing my best war paint

Lashes and lip liner, foundation caked

Waterproof mascara for when the tears overtake

Not worried about a black eye or bloody lip

Hearts don't break by a physical hit

Good thing my heart is the same size as my fist

Not a physical swing, but you'll feel when I hit

Because I fight using everything I've got within

And that's a lot of passion

Rocky told us how to win

It's not about how hard we can hit

It's about how hard we can take it

And still move forward, that's true grit

It's fighting from victory, not for it

Always a lesson, never a loss

Be proud of yourself, you still fought

When you fight with hope and faith

It's okay to leave the ring with heartache

Or lay on the ropes, absorbing change

Life challenges are never-ending

Another round, ding ding

Spiritual Discipline

Never fully absent of the enemy

Sin will always be surrounding

Look at Adam and Eve

Set in paradise

Even this beautiful place had a parasite

Learning how to walk in faith, not by sight

Faith gives us the strength to fight

Our hearts crave sin, we're human

Resisting temptations is a battle within

Not to let the enemy win

It takes spiritual discipline

When we chose to lean on Him

Guidance comes to fruition

Listen as He speaks, hear every word

Substances won't take away your hurt

Scales can't measure your worth

Mirror reflections don't preserve

Your smile is your best curve

Love & Kindness, God Armor

Mona Lisa Series Intro

The message being conveyed in this series, using Mona Lisa metaphorically, is symbolic to the idea that we are all masterpieces.

Although we were not painted by Leonardo da Vinci, and our portraits aren't known world-wide or displayed in a museum —

We have a different creator.

We are all works of art created by God. We are His work in progress and masterpiece.

No one else is you, and that is your power.

This series intends to honor individuality, we are each one-of-a-kind.

God designed.

"For we are God's masterpiece. He has created us anew in Christ Jesus, so we can do the good things He planned for us long ago."

EPHESIANS 2:10

Human Masterpiece

Judging our own flaws, weaknesses and sins
Leaves us often discouraged, lost in comparison
Desiring to be different, more like her or him
Envying the traits we admire in them

Growth into self-discovery is a transformation
Dig deeper, your power lies within
It's that no body else in the world is you
Developing a sense of identity, true value
Like Leonardo's Mona Lisa —
you're a masterpiece too
One-of-a-kind, God's design, created beautiful
Characteristics personalized and intentional
Distinctive qualities that make you special
Gifts we can use to bless others

Illuminate the qualities you were born with
To walk in freedom and fulfill your purpose
We're all human, no one is perfect
Bring it all together, simultaneously
You're His work in progress and masterpiece

Every shade

He painted the depths of our traits

Discover your inner strength

To step out of frame

Mona Lisa masterpiece, modern day

Mona Lisa

Considered a masterpiece
Painted by Leonardo da Vinci

Notion of happiness
Grinning modestly
Demeanor serene
Novel qualities

Dressed in Florentine Fashion
Wearing the best enigmatic expression
Subtle presence,
Monumental composition
Calming posture
Amongst a landscape vision

Linking nature and humanity
An inclination of overall harmony

Unheard silence behind her faint smile,
"Mona Lisa is a living quandary
Her soul is depicted, but inaccessible"

Nature Of Uniqueness

Observe the environment's layers

Living examples of variety in nature

Numerous species, all unique

Complimenting each other perfectly

Combining into a beautiful vision

Celebration of differences,

Every form of nature, fully authentic

He delights in our individuality and uniqueness

Created independently for a purpose

Symbolic Reflection

Iris depicts Mona Lisa's reflection

Symbolic we're all masterpieces

Not da Vinci's, but God's creation

Blended hues on the surface

Beneath our skin, bones form a skeleton

Reminder we're all human

Experiencing joy and pain,

We all bleed the same

We all bleed
the same

Inner Child Series Intro

This series is a reminder of how important our inner child is, even as adults.

During active addiction, my sensitivity was numbed and I grew more and more distant from the little girl I once was.

This series challenges you to remember to yourself as a child, before the world hurt you and your heart became a little colder.

How would you operate differently to protect and nurture your innocence, with the wisdom you have now?

I guarantee this thought, if put into action, would bring you closer to your authentic self — which the world tends to pull us further away from. But we have the power to reconnect.

*"And anyone who welcomes a little child
like this on my behalf is welcoming me."*

MATTHEW 18"5

Euphoric Recall

Life happens

Unpredictable and unexpected

Situations can lead to an explosion

Of an internal sensory disruption

Spiraling negative thoughts

Make the emotional bleeding stop

The real me doesn't feel seen at all

Who is she? Lost my inner child

Euphoric recall

Feelings of sensitivity to numb

Chemical dependency: emotional shut off

Romanticizing the instantaneous shift

Never really trusted

Mentally flip the switch

Secrets keep you sick

Inner Child

The little girl I used to be

My inner child staring back at me

Crooked bangs and a gap between her teeth

Wide-eyed and smiling wondrously

An innocent outlook, magic in simplicity

Substances buried you slowly

And I disregarded your existence within me

You watched me use, it shattered you

Grateful you've never disappeared completely

Reminding me I didn't always
need this to be happy

Asking me if I can hear Mom sobbing

Give me your hand, I'll keep you safe

This is a new chapter for us to navigate

I'm sober now, let's heal the pain

Trust my gut feeling, intuitive instinct

You can sense oncoming heartache

Promise I'll keep them at arm's length

I'm fighting our demons again, feeling tempted

Play the tape forward, you know how this ends

You have my word, I won't go there again

Show me the world through your lens

I want my inner child to last

Self-discovery as an adult is leading me back

To you

ℬLOSSOM

This poem connects the idea of growth in recovery to a flower.

Like a flower begins beneath the ground, it has to grow through the dirt to blossom into it's true beauty.

Through recovery and healing, we tend to truly bloom in this process.

"But the word of God continued to spread and flourish."

ACTS 12:24

BLOOM

There's solitude within the soil,

The thoughts planted in my mind

I grow a garden within my imagination,

It feels safer to keep inside;

Protected within my heart,

from a world that's hurt too many times

Then I find myself mesmerized

by a flower blooming in the sunshine —

Once hidden beneath the earth,

rooted in the dirt,

Waiting patiently for a storm,

it needed the rain —

Talk about embracing change

What if I can find the strength?

What if I have enough faith?

To learn from my mistakes,

Allow myself to feel the pain —

Find the source of water within the hurricane

Now I am sober, no longer numb,

Ready to grow and truly blossom

What can I do for the kingdom?

As my mind wonders on —
I leave my last question with God

The thoughts
planted in my
mind. I grow a
garden within my
imagination

Ashtray

This poem is an effort to quit my last vice, smoking cigarettes.

I reminisce back to my first cigarette, and end the poem with 'ashtray' to imply my last.

Smoking, like many substances, is addictive and not good for our health; however it is a hard habit to kick.

I went back in time to remember my first cigarette

"The Lord's enemies are like flowers in a field — they will disappear like smoke"

PSALMS 37:20

ASHTRAY

People talk about dancing in the rain;

Judging by my self-destructive ways,

I've been playing in the flames

I haven't always been this way

First time, first heartbreak

I didn't know how to handle the pain

High school, starting to party days

There were a lot of firsts in that,
not just a cigarette

Gave from the bottom of my heart, to the bed

As life went by, my biggest regret —

Experimenting with ways to escape my mind

We're drawn to light, it's the human eye

Along with many things that we
can't explain why

My solution and best form of therapy:

Light one up

But I was only hurting me

I know 'smoking is bad', but not the feeling

The action can't be worse than my reasons

I tried anything to fight the inner demons

These ashes know my secrets

It's time to let go

Of all my crutches and hidden sins,
take a good look within

There are bad habits I can't seem to break,

a list of character defects that I hate

But I'll admit, I know it's time —
throw it all into the fire

As it burns, I'll refine

A new decision as I make the choice,

to no longer ignite flames that can destroy

But to rekindle an old flame,
with who I once was

Before the world hurt too much

Still fascinated by fire, now I just carry a lighter

Always in my pocket

Thumb on the wheel, I love to spark it

Hold the smoke

You can only sweep so much under a rug
Until it begins to show

As I set something new ablaze,
It's the passion of purpose that's within my soul

Hopeful that it will spread through me:
The fire of love in my heart,
purification as I cleanse,
transformation as I grow
The refining process starts within

I'll never forget where I've been
Lost in the smoke, but never alone
He reminds me I've always been whole

Like a metal that's been through heat & flames —
pure and reflective as it shines
My heart continues to be refined
In the fire, to be sober and clear was my desire
No longer amongst smokey mirrors

I can't do this solo, please hold me close

To God I pray

Help me change my ways

Last cigarette. Ashtray

Like a metal that's been through heat & flames — pure and reflective as it shines. My heart continues to be refined

ꞴETTY ꞘORD

This poem was written when I was extremely tempted to relapse during my current sobriety journey.

I made it to 6 months, and instead of pursuing my thoughts of relapsing into action, I wrote a poem about the first time I did relapse during my first recovery attempt.

This helped me play the tape forward and make the decision it's not worth ruining my progress on this journey.

"No one who is human can be truly pure and righteous"

JOB 15:14

Betty Ford

Enticed by lust, driven by pride

Denying my ego would be a lie

When temptations lead, it's misguiding

Demons in disguise surrounding

Grateful for the Angels standing right behind me

It's up to me to make the call,

If I'm wrong, trust fall?

One side says: one more time, keep it a secret

The other side reminds me I'll repeat it

But it's right in front of me, so inviting

I'm shy of one month clean

How selfish can you be

Enabling someone you love to live carelessly

It can't just be a one-time thing,

Not for me.

It doesn't work that way.

Fuck it, let's get high

This will be the 'last time'

I'm by no means perfect,

Please don't kick a person

Who's already down

Are you reading this right now?

Behind your mask of righteousness

A red nose would be a little more accurate

Please don't try to make amends

Ask Siri to call Hazelden

Diaries of an addict,

I'm still human.

ANGEL

This poem was written due to lack of confidence to recover out loud.

Sharing my recovery and sobriety can feel scary at times, you wonder who's judging you and what people will think about you.

This poem reminds me of someone I loved and lost due to substance abuse.

It's a reminder that sharing your story can help others, and I gain my strength to speak up through this Angel I wrote about.

"For He will order His angels to protect you wherever you go."

PSALMS 91:11

ANGEL

What's it like to touch the sky?
I've always wanted to fly

People buy roses for the fresh scent;
And hold on to perished ones that
hold remembrance

It's been a few years, have you witnessed
The living diaries of my addictions?
Recovering out loud can knock my confidence
Then there you are again
We share another cigarette

You don't judge me, you understand
And I love to see that beaming grin
Angel, lover, and friend

Rainbow after a tear shower
I wish I could sleep a little longer
After we meet in my dreams
I wake up with a voice to speak

Coming Undone

This poem was written based on a music video costume I wore for a song I helped artists Zhaklina and Hollow Wake co-write called 'Game Over.'

For this costume scene, I was wrapped within a fabric cocoon, which represented my the mental trap of shame and addiction.

This project helped propel me into my healing journey as I became aware of the importance of mental health relating to addiction.

I became sober while filming this project and this poem represents that feeling of being trapped and 'coming undone.'

"And the dead man came out, his hands and feet bound in graveclothes, his face wrapped in head cloth."

Jesus told them, "unwrap him and let him go!"

JOHN 11:44

COMING UNDONE

Wrapped within a mastered art of chaos

Disaster can be so gorgeous

Heavy clouds and smoke

I prefer to design beauty, form it into my own

Sink into the depths of shadows

A fascinating story to be told

Physically distant, but connect with your soul

Nature demonstrates nothing can stay

The seasons change

And we are reborn

Most captivating part of a storm

Is the freedom of the wind

Everything comes undone, then you start again

Disaster
can be so
gorgeous

Shadow Dancing

This poem was written during another intense craving and feelings of depression.

I realized these feelings come from feeling suffocated by negativity.

This negativity lives in our minds as we can spiral mentally, feeling overwhelmed by shadows of criticism.

Self-criticism, and the voice of others.

From past experiences to future fears.

This poem is a reminder that we can still dance amongst the shadows.

Eventually the darkness dissipates, and we can rise above these shadows.

Leaning into Our Father during dark times can help us through, imagining we are under the darkness of His wing — protected, safe, and loved.

"How precious is your unfailing love, O God! All humanity finds shelter in the shadow of your wings"

PSALMS 36:7

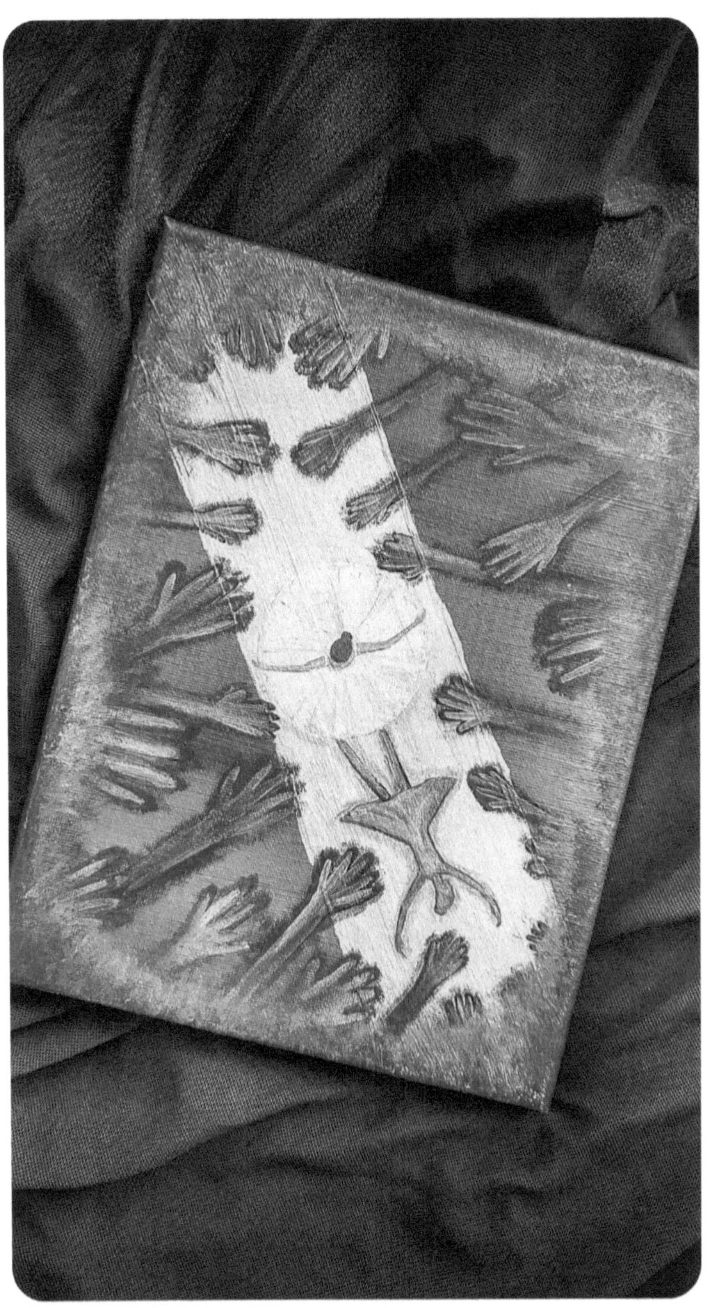

SHADOWS

Shadows that follow

From a place within me that's hollow

Suffocating the light

My shadows collide

Eventually the darkness overtakes

Pain that's stayed

Remembering the love I gave

But it was never deserved

Let my thoughts set flames

Watch it burn

Feel the warmth

Like fire, I become stronger than before

Masochist from the hurt

Ashes thrown in my direction

Foundation for my transformation

Pain beneath the dirt, my personal collection

Emerging with a new perspective

Like a phoenix rising, majestic

Dancing in darkness

Beneath the shadow of Your wings

Wind-up doll

Cut the puppet strings

SOAR

This poem is about finding ourselves in the midst of chaos.

And rising above the shadows casted upon us by the world and ourselves.

It's about falling into God's arms and rising above all else.

Discovering and understanding yourself through His eternal love for you, His child.

"But those who trust in the Lord will find new strength.
They will soar high on wings like eagles.
They will run and not grow weary.
They will walk and not faint."

ISAIAH 40:31

SOAR

Tough times eventually reveal

What good times conceal

Encountering difficulties unexpectedly

Causing fear and uncertainty

Shadows move amongst

Refusing to let them rise above

Used to fear endings, seeming so tragic

But the healing process is pure magic

Seeing God at work in the messiness

Helping you face strong headwinds

And rise to new heights, wings spread

With an elevated perspective

Faith can anchor your soul

in the midst of the storm.

Maintaining your momentum forward

With the ability to be agile and shift course

Allow His heart to speak into yours

And soar

Recovery is about the life we create

One we don't want to escape

But the healing process is pure magic